# LEARNER-MANAGED LEARNING

## Edited by Paul Ginnis

Education Now Books

Published 1992 by Education Now Publishing Co-operative,
P.O. Box 186, Ticknall, Derbyshire, DE7 1WF

Copyright © 1992 Copyright enquiries to Education Now Publishing Co-operative

British Library Cataloguing in Publication Data
A catalogue record for this book is available from the British Library

ISBN 1-871526-08-6

This book is sold subject to the condition that it shall not, by way of trade or otherwise, be lent, re-sold, hired out, or otherwise circulated without the publisher's prior consent in any form of binding or cover other than that in which it is published and without a similar condition including this condition being imposed on the subsequent purchaser.

Design: Computer Graphics Enterprise
Printed in Great Britain by:
Computer Graphics Enterprise, Nottingham

# Introduction

*by Paul Ginnis*

I remember some time ago telling a colleague of mine how much I had enjoyed a lecture by a leading educationalist. 'Yes, but he's still saying the same things he's said for years' was the biting reply. For a while I was silenced by this remark, hardly daring to speak to anyone until I'd got some new ideas. But, I couldn't really think of any - and still can't!

This book is likely to disappoint my colleague. Essentially, it rehearses ideas that have been established for many years, although their applications are current. There is, I believe, actually nothing more powerful to say about education than this: that all people, however young or old, have an enormous drive and capacity to learn; that many aspects of typical schooling get in the way of this, partly by assuming that the reverse is true; that learners really start to explore and exercise their potential only as they take charge of their lives; that the most effective teachers trust learners, enhance their self-esteem, have no need to control them, provide unconditional support which doesn't go too far, and value all types of intelligence in all areas of learning.

## What is learner-managed learning?

The term 'learner-managed learning' leads us into some difficulty. It is used to describe approaches which encourage or require learners to take responsibility for their learning, and is common in all phases of education. However, as an umbrella term it can disguise important differences between various types of practice, even the ones found within this book. Perhaps the most crucial differences, which need to be examined openly, are the *degree* to which students' responsibility for learning is recognised, and the *degree* to which this recognition affects the teachers' behaviour and the structures within which the learning takes place, for example the organisation of the school, the course, the assessment, and all the 'norms' that create formal and informal routines.

Some time ago I used to get teachers to do a training exercise which I've since dropped because they told me it made them feel guilty. If you're willing to run the risk, you could have a go for yourself. Bring to mind a piece of teaching that you were pleased with - a lesson, a project or a course - and ask yourself who took responsibility for *planning, organising, doing* and *assessing* the learning. Now plot the position of these four elements on a continuum from the teacher taking full responsibility for them to the students being fully responsible.

What pattern emerges? With groups of teachers, both primary and secondary, I used to find that organising, doing and assessing would be variously positioned according to the teacher's style ... and almost always planning would be towards the teacher's end.

When the idea was pushed a bit further and teachers were asked 'Yes, but who *actually took responsibility* for the planning, organising, doing and assessing? That is, who initiated them, who made sure they happened, or happened in a particular way or by a particular time?' Who chivvied the students along for example? Then I found that all four aspects tended to creep towards the teacher's end. Dare I ask what would happen in your case?

In a *fully* learner-managed or, in my terms student-centred, setting students would be making all the key decisions - the ones teachers usually make - about tasks, deadlines, resources, who to work with, what record to keep, how to assess and so on. And, significantly, they would be initiating the need to make these decisions. The learners would be regarded as having charge of their own lives. They would be viewed as responsible for their achievements, their behaviour, their participation, their feelings and their futures .... and would be held responsible for each, without excuse. Far from being laissez faire, this is a tough approach in which no one is let off the hook. There are examples of it working successfully with learners of all ages, although I am most familiar with its application to the secondary years. (1)

## Going the whole hog

Teachers are used to exercising more control than this, however, and it is not surprising that the approach is rather too radical for most people. Demanding as it is, this student-centred approach has a sound rationale. It acknowledges simple truths about human being, for example, that people can't be given responsibility for learning, they automatically and always have it. Any individual can resist internalising ideas and facts, even under threat, or can choose to let them in; learning is always an act of the learner's, not the teacher's, will. All people have tremendous personal power, they naturally posess curiosity and readily acquire a range of learning skills. People have a tendency to resent being told what to do, when to do it, how it must be done and why. People are most open to new ideas when their self-esteem is high, when they are believed in and feel secure with the people around them. People work hardest when they have a genuine stake in the outcome and have themselves made key decisions about the process. People are always *whole* people, they are always feeling as well as thinking; intuition, laughter, irrational as well as rational thought are all part of human wellbeing and each has its place in the learning process.

Teachers and schools ignore these truths at their peril, but ignore them they usually do, partly because of the deep traditions of authoritarianism and behaviourism in British schooling (I would say that the student-centred approach is anti-behaviourist), partly because of the expediencies of managing inhumanly-sized schools, partly because of fear, partly because - you add your own.

## Variations on the theme

Although the fully fledged method is frequently dismissed, more 'limited' (if I may call them that) forms of learner-managed learning are widespread. The limitation is in the degree of choice offered to learners. Ask: how much choice do they have? Over what do they have it? How often do learners have choice? How many decisions are made for them before they are asked to have their say? Who created the choices for them in the first place?

The so-called child-centred practice of many primary schools is often cited as an example. As for secondary and tertiary education, the Eighties turned out to be a decade of major change. A plethora of overlapping initiatives, each claiming to be learner-managed in character, was launched. The regional flexible learning projects, established by (what was) the Training Agency in 1989 under the aegis of the Technical and Vocational Education Initiative, could be said to summarise these innovations inasmuch as they promote many key features of their practice. Consequently, the flexible learning framework (as it is called) could be regarded as a paradigm for a set of approaches now common in the education of 14-18 year olds and similar to many features of primary practice.

A flexible learning situation is officially defined as one in which "students:
- identify and understand the objectives and goals of the course;
- negotiate with teachers and peers, learning targets and work out the most effective ways of achieving them;
- are able to build personally relevant goals into target setting;
- work more often in small groups and teams on realistic tasks and will have to resolve problems and make decisions in order to complete these tasks;
- have direct access to a range of learning resources other than the teacher;
- get specific and individually relevant feedback from a variety of sources on which they can reflect, identify strengths and weaknesses and take appropriate action;
- regularly review progress with the teacher and peers and thus develop self-evaluation skills;
- work to short term targets in the context of longer term goals;
- develop the skills of working with and supporting others, through small group and team work;
- identify and use support from a number of sources and in a variety of contexts." (2)

## What's the difference?

There are many similarities between this description and the fully student-centred approach described earlier - at least on the surface. At times the practice would look identical. But what of the underlying purposes? Flexible learning claims to be "important because, by the nature of the learning processes involved, young people are better equipped for the demands of working life in a rapidly changing, highly technological society" (3) and "unless people in work have these (personal effectiveness) competencies, the whole nation will be the poorer." (4)

However, most major developments flying the flag of learner-managed learning, did not set out to solve the problems of a capitalist economy panicking in the throes of recession and technological overhaul. Rather, their motives were rooted in very different philosophical soils, based on the bedrock ideas of major figures such as John Holt, Carl Rogers, Ivan Illich, Paolo Freire, Abraham Maslow, A.S. Neill, John Dewey, Montessori, Pestalozzi, through to Rousseau (in part) and even back to Socrates. The list is endless and largely comprises libertarians, humanistic psychologists and holistic philosophers. Together, they tend to the non-totalitarian Left and some are politically explicit.

Carl Rogers, for example, is clear about the implications of student-centred teaching:

"It is not education which would be relevant in an authoritarian philosophy. If the aim of education is to produce well-informed technicians who will be completely amenable to carrying out all orders of consituted authority without questioning, then the method .... .is highly inappropriate. In general it is relevant only to the type of goal which is loosely described as democratic." (5)

He goes on: " .... the goal of democratic education is to assist students to become individuals

- who are able to take self-initiated action and to be responsible for those actions;
- who are capable of intelligent choice and self-direction;
- who are critical learners, able to evaluate the contributions made by others;
- who have acquired knowledge relevant to the solution of problems;
- who, even more importantly, are able to adapt flexibly and intelligently to new problem situations;
- who have internalized an adaptive mode of approach to problems, utilising all pertinent experience freely and creatively;
- who are able to co-operate effectively with others in these various activities;
- who work, not for the apporoval of others, but in terms of their own socialised purposes." (6)

How does this list compare to the description of flexible learning above? The differences are subtle, yet betray quite distinct attitudes to the purpose of education. In Rogers there is a feeling of students becoming assertive and critically aware. There is a sense of self-direction for the sake of self, rather than society and of students knowing how to achieve what they want in life. This contrasts with an approach which seems to want to harness rather than unleash personal effectiveness, which prepares students for pseudo - rather than true democracy, an approach in which learning is repackaged, but remains as prescriptive and restrictive as ever.

There is something different, but not radical, about styles of learner-managed learning which fit the 'flexible learning' paradigm.

They are, I believe, a more effective way of doing what was done before. Compared to didactic approaches, they require new techniques and they do result in significant learning through process as well as content. Personal and social skills are clearly developed alongside 'subject' learning. Consequently, these approaches are to be welcomed. They attempt to rid the system of some toxic practices and add many benefits. But, how big are the ideas behind them? What do they challenge? What would have to change for them to flourish? What kind of society would they create?

## Shaking the foundations

Some teachers have been reluctant to accept even the mildest of these changes. Others have seen the various initiatives as opportunities to bring about unintended changes, as chances to realise bigger visions, and have sought to subvert the official purpose. But, when all is said and done, the 'limited' forms still fit neatly into schools and society as they currently exist. Teachers who have grander ideas, then have a problem. They come up against the self-preserving System, in the form of power, people and procedures. So, they either learn to live with dissonance and disillusionment or they leave, looking for more conducive environments and in some cases, new careers entirely.

There are examples (Hartshill School in Nuneaton is one) of grant-maintained schools exercising their new-found freedom to create organisational conditions favourable to learners' self-management. However, they are still bounded by statutory requirements and, in most cases, by the slow-to-change attitudes of staff, Governors, parents and, of course, students who may not know what it is to be self-directing. This is the lot of any state school, however visionary the Head.

By contrast, it is easy to operate learner-managed learning outside the state System. Libertarian-influenced schools in the independent sector have an ideal opportunity to exemplify the practice and articulate it to the public. This is a good time for them to reconsider their position, as for example The King Alfred School in London is doing, and assess the contribution they could make to popular and professional views. Home educators too are perfectly placed to show the way in what, to them, is a natural style.

This is a time to shake the foundations of the Right's proud new structure and the profession's sleepy acceptance of it. The prescriptive

National Curriculum and its narrow assessments are bullying teachers into an increasingly didactic frame of mind while public exposure, market forces and doctrinaire attacks on almost any form of non-traditional teaching all conspire to frighten schools away from ideas which might jeopardise their results. Some teachers are now too tired, while others are busily building their unquestioning careers on the back of the reforms. Few have the conviction or the strength, it seems, to counter the bulldozer-like effect of statutory change.

Learner-managed learning, if taken to anything like its logical conclusion, is radical .... and resisted. It is now up to 'the converted' in the System and out of it, for both are needed, to collaborate in presenting the irresistable common sense of this natural way to teach and learn.

**References**

1. Brandes, D and Ginnis, P (1986) *A Guide to Student-Centred Learning* (Oxford, Blackwell) and (1990) *The Student-Centred School* (Oxford, Blackwell)

2. *Flexible Learning: A Framework for Education and Training in the Skills Decade* (TVEI Unit, Employment Department, Moorfoot, Sheffield) (1991) p.16

3. op. cit. p.12  4. *op cit* p.4

4. Rogers, C (1951) *Client-Centred Therapy* (London, Constable) p.387

5. *op cit* pp.387-388

*Paul* is a freelance educational consultant and part-time advisory teacher with Birmingham Education Authority.

# Acquiring Skills for Learner-managed Learning by Research Projects

*by Mike Roberts*

What happens when sixth form students are free from the constraints of examination syllabuses? How do they manage when teacher control is removed? How skilled are they in making decisions about their own learning? What skills are required?

Data for this report, based on my PhD thesis, was provided by 52 students from Tameside Comprehensive school (TS) and Colebank Sixth form College (CB) (fictitious names for real institutions) who conducted research for their AEB General Studies projects. They were given eight months to plan, gather, process and present their information with minimal guidance from supervising taechers. I have assembled the following taxonomy of skills from their experiences.

## Planning skills

Having negotiated a research topic with the teacher, students constructed written Proposals, their long-term research plans for the ensuing six months. Skilful planning meant proposing viable activities, yet only 31% of students implemented their plans fully. Reflective skill involving projection was required, but:

> *"they are not practised at seeing implications of things in advance, at anticipating...."* **(Colebank teacher)**

Used skilfully, Proposals served as action checklists giving students a sense of future direction:

> *"I've done that - what must I do next?"* **(Nermin CB)**

Skilful long-term planners defined clear aims focussed as specific objectives or questions:

> *"How do Junior Schools and Secondary Schools differ? I aim to examine and illustrate the difference which pupils aged eleven experience in the move from Junior to Secondary School."* **(Lorraine TS)**

While 'investigators' constructed specific objectives from the outset, others clarified aims en route which guided subsequent information gathering. Students who could not start lacked the direction which such aims would have provided:

> *"It is difficult because I don't know exactly what I'm looking for."*

*(Hitesh CB)*

Operationalising Proposals into action was a critical skill which entailed knowing how to, and being able to, extract from Proposals a series of action plans for organising their information search in the short-run. Some received guidance in defining actions required:

> *"They need help in being specific and selective ...."*
> *(Tameside teacher)*

Skilful students could propose a series of specific tasks for the next 2-4 weeks:

> *"Next I will find out what a typical day is like for these children. I will do a case study of one particular child and take photographs of the school, the grounds, the children at work ...."*
> *(Lisa TS)*

With purpose and direction they made progress by implementing such action plans. Those without these skills were aimless. Not knowing what to do next they either postponed action, which resulted in time management problems later, or they required intervention from teachers.

Planning also required students to respond to problems. Self-appraisal skill contributed to the recognition of a problem and its accurate diagnosis. Reflective skill enabled a strategy or solution to be devised. One student reduced the scope of his project upon realising that his Proposal to examine the 'Arab-Israeli Conflict' was too ambitious. Without the former skill students could be unaware of a problem e.g. by half-time six students had not started, yet had not recognised that they were in trouble.

## Gathering skills

Students ranked gathering information by field research as the most difficult and complex project activity. It demanded interpersonal skills. Communication by telephone, letter or in person was required for students to negotiate initial access to field locations. For making first contact with strangers, who were frequently authority figures, communication skill was necessary:

> *"It was the first time I interviewed people (social worker, police officer) in such positions. Because of this I was nervous ...."*
> *(Nermin CB)*

The skilful knew how to introduce themselves, explain their purpose and ask for assistance. Social skills were employed in coaxing strangers; remaining patient yet persisting until requests were granted. Developing rapport with field contacts also meant:

*".... they've got to sell themselves to make it seem worthwhile ... they've got to have social graces, the 'pleases' and 'thank yous'." (Tameside teacher)*

Approaching fieldwork skilfully meant being well prepared e.g. briefed for interview by extensive background reading. It also meant approaching strangers with clear aims and a sense of purpose. Such dynamism in dialogue required skill in keeping the initiative, however:

*"I ended up scrapping my questions. Once I got there he started talking - I didn't ask any more." (Ian TS)*

Students needed technical skills in designing and using instruments for social research e.g. questionnaires. No reading in research methods was undertaken and skills were rare as students improvised. Inappropriate instruments were used with questions irrelevant or ambiguous as

*"I didn't know what sort of questions to ask." (Suresh CB)*

Some displayed opportunist skill which demanded perception to recognise an information gathering opportunity and inter-personal skill to manage its exploitation e.g. an impromptu interview with the Foreman whilst visiting a WMPTE bus depot. The self-aware exploited themselves or families as information sources, but some missed the opportunity. Several were unable to ask supplementary questions in interview because they lacked the skill to improvise questions in situ.

Adaptive skills were required in response to fieldwork problems. This could mean seeking information from alternative sources or modifying methods of gathering e.g. Richard TS switched from a postal questionnaire to a direct survey of fans at the football ground when none of the former were returned.

For students who gathered information by reading, library-use skills were advantageous. However, some could not search, locate and select relevant books. Lorraine TS, who complained "there's nothing on Education in the school library", was unable to use the subject index which might have led her to 250 such books. Reference library skills were deficient also:

*"I had to take him to the reference section and show him the books on the shelves." (Colebank teacher)*

On more familiar territory most students had a range of book-use skills. They were able to select appropriate information to read, use and note, although "deciding what's relevant" was not easy. While most possessed paraphrasing skills, some plagiarised, perhaps lacking other skills e.g.:

> "Mostly I copied because I thought it would save time and I would get the important points which were there in the book .... "
> (Jagtar CB)

**Processing skills**

Skliful processors applied their own interpretations, analyses, evaluations and judgements to raw information gathered - they used it to draw their own conclusions.

Skilful processing transformed information by subjecting it to analysis e.g. Paul TS compared 13 chess sets having devised his own criteria. Where material read was processed, new meaning was created through reflection as students offered opinions and commentaries of their own:

> "I used to believe that youngsters who committed crime are to be blamed but when I learned the reasons I don't blame them so much.... " (Nermin CB)

Using information creatively required cognitive reasoning skills including evaluation, making judgements, drawing conclusions and recognising concepts and conceptual connections e.g. having evaluated official programmes of several football clubs, one student reached the following concept-embodying conclusion:

> "Manchester United's programme was the best but also the cheapest. Success does not mean that one has to pay more."
> (Richard TS)

Four 'investigators' manipulated their analysed information to answer questions posed earlier. Processing skill was instrumental in producing answers e.g. the student investigating 'Transition from Junior to Secondary School' concluded:

> ".... upheaval for children to change schools. They have to make new friends, become accustomed to an immense building, study new subjects .... a very anxious time for Junior pupils."
> (Lorraine TS)

Reflective self-reporting was a processing skill. One student employed self-analysis in speculating about the origin of his interest in cricket. In another case, evaluating material read against personal experience produced:

> *"It is said that as soon as pupils leave the classroom they revert to Creole. I find this statement unjust .... being born and brought up in Birmingham I would be more likely to speak with a 'Brummie' accent."* **(Marcia CB)**

Such effective reporting of considered personal feelings or experiences was unusual.

### Presenting skills

Students asserted that presentation was the least difficult project activity.

Structuring skill meant first that students created their own chapter structure, including sub-heads and contents order. The unskilled followed external sources like textbooks e.g. one student plagiarised 16 sub-sections. Second, the skilful developed a coherent theme by connecting chapters logically e.g. chapters on 'Delinquency', 'Juvenile Courts' and 'Treatment' followed offenders chronologically from crime to punishment. Unskilled structuring presented a mass of information in isolated or numerous chapters. Third, skilful student 'investigators' achieved unity of introduction, project body and conclusion. This skill was deficient among others e.g. 8 students had no conclusion.

Students wrote an average of 32.5 sides of A4 in finished projects. Writing skills of summary, synthesis and paraphrasing were widespread, reflecting years of experience.

Where illustrations were employed effectively to exemplify points in the text contextual skill was evident, but some illustrated gratuitously, without comment or context, creating a 'scrap-book' effect.

Those with artistic skills of graphic design and freehand drawing exploited them.

Bibliographical skills of presenting complete, accurate, detailed listings of sources were deficient.

### Time management skills

Having to manage their time for a submission deadline eight months ahead required several skills.

First, it meant budgeting sufficient time and organising themselves to implement plans by commencing information gathering early. Unskilled students started so late that fieldwork plans were adapted, or abandoned by 13 Colebank students e.g.:

*"I had to change my plan to something I could do in the time left." (Marcia CB)*

Skill entailed both making time available for project work in competition with other subject demands, and utilising available time efficiently e.g.:

*"I had time in the Christmas holiday so I got down to it." (David TS)*

Unskilled time managers were still gathering when they should have been writing up - 32 students failed to meet submission deadlines.

Second, for time budgeting students had to estimate gathering times skilfully. some were incapable of realistic timescale estimates e.g. to plan, design, produce, distribute, collect and process questionnaires. Fieldwork was underprepared, hurried or abandoned in consequence. Over presentation:

*"Some wore themselves out near the deadline writing it up." (Angela TS)*

Photographs, tape recordings and other artefacts were omitted in the rush.

Third, as time progressed, skilful management meant being realistic about the amount of gathering feasible in the time remaining. Six Colebank students failed to execute new fieldwork planned for the final month.

Students learned dearly that time was a constraint.

## Some Implications

Many students were skill deficient and required help from supervising teachers, whose role will be discussed elsewhere. Not all sought help. Some drifted. Unable to manage, they dropped out. Ten students did not submit finished projects.

Fieldwork and reading offered contrasting learning experiences. Fieldwork involved organising access and establishing contact with a wider, more diverse range of information sources, using people which are primary sources rather than books which are secondary ones. It also meant operating in external locations rather than traditional school or college libraries. As a novel experience for most students, and since it offered more scope for learner decision-making, fieldwork was more demanding of skills.

Who were the most skilful? The projects of 'investigators' like Nermin and Richard who constructed specific objectives, converged as they developed. Their questions directed information gathering which became progressively more focussed as it proceeded. Processing was instrumental in providing answers and conclusions to their questions. From their finished projects clear themes emerged. Some of their skills were independent.

Projects of less skilful students diverged. Commencing with broad Proposals like 'Television' they so lacked clarity of aim that information gathering was unfocussed. They gathered information on a broad front which grew in diversity, and which they simply reported 'unprocessed'. Clear themes were indistinguishable in finished projects e.g. Heena CB presented an unstructured data mountain on 'Advertising'.

It may be possible to use skill concepts in a diagnostic way. For each skill a 'skill possessed' - 'no skill' continuum may be envisaged. By making a subjective assessment of the degree of skill acquired, it would be possible to position a learner on each continuum. An overall profile of an individual's skills might thus be obtained at any stage, along with improvements or 'acquisitions' over time. Might such profiles be used by learners to diagnose how skilful they were in managing their own learning?

Students who genuinely managed their own projects seemed well motivated:

> "I think the project is great. I find that every time I ask questions and find something out, I have another question .... I've never enjoyed working so much." (Angela TS)

It is suggested here that skills were necessary, but did motivation follow skill acquisition or vice versa? Does autonomy follow skill acquisition or vice versa? The skills-autonomy-motivation relationship begs further investigation.

Mike's PhD thesis will shortly be submitted to the University of Birmingham and is expected to be available in the Faculty of

Education library from January 1993.

Mike is Vice Principal of Cadbury Sixth form College, Birmingham.

# Student-centred Drama - the Art of Learning

*by Sharon Robinson*

I have been interested for some time now in the natural connection, as I see it, between student-centred learning and drama. At one time I focused on obvious similarities such as a shared belief in the power of groupwork, and the practice of collaboration and negotiation. But as an artist I knew that this didn't go far enough to explain the intuitive excitement I felt about the student-centred philosophy. I now believe that fundamental purposes of both drama-in-education and student-centred learning are to foster people's natural creativity, and to support individuality and autonomy. I have discovered that the process of learning in drama can be accelerated by adopting a student-centred approach.

My latest reflections on how I can work with learners in a way which honours these beliefs, are best illustrated by describing two pieces of my teaching. The two lessons were attempts at supporting learner-managed learning in drama. As it turned out, one was more appropriate than the other, given the previous experience of the children, and this helped me clarify what I believe are the essential foundations for the learner-managed approach.

The first lesson was with a class of four year olds. The starting point for this drama was a large blank sheet of sugar paper. I told them that we were going to make a story together and asked them to help me draw where the story would take place. One child told me to draw a house, which I did. I asked who lived in the house but no one answered. I asked where the house was and someone said it was at the seaside. I suggested the house might be an hotel but one child wanted to be in a caravan, two or three others also wanted to be in caravans and drew them on to the paper. I asked if anyone was going to be in a tent and two or three said they were. I was thinking about possible scenarios which would provide something to act out at this point. I picked up my old straw hat which I often use to start drama sessions and told the children that when I put the hat on I was going to pretend to be the person who lived in the house and I also owned the caravan park. I asked them to pretend they were on holiday at my park.

I decided to begin the drama with everyone pretending to be on a beach. Working in role as the holiday park owner, I welcomed them to the park and showed them down the cliff path to the sea. While we were acting out beach activities such as paddling and building sandcastles I kept my mind open to any ideas the children wanted to add to the story. The children didn't add any new ideas at this point, so using my role as the park owner I asked them if they would help me design and build a play area for children staying on the site. We drew a plan and then acted out building. I decided to heighten the emotional engagement the children had with the story by adding a point of tension, so I took my hat off, signalling that I was coming out of role, and stopped the drama. I told them they had all been asleep and that when the story started again it would be early next morning. I put my hat on again and told them that, sadly, someone had smashed up the play area we had built the day before. I asked if anyone had heard anything in the night. This was the idea that caught their attention and imagination.

There had been enough dramatic action by now for them to understand a little about the way drama works, that it involved pretending, and acting out, and that they had an open invitation to collaborate with me to devise the story. Someone felt confident enough to say that a person had come into their caravan but it was too dark to see them. Others had heard noises. I suggested we looked for clues, the group carefully looked around the classroom. Then a child told me that Snoopy was missing. I didn't know who or what Snoopy was but I called the group back together and the two of us told them all that Snoopy was missing. Another child said Snoopy was in a cave tied up. I said we'd have to be careful because the person who took Snoopy might catch us. We all acted out sneaking down to the cave. I stopped the drama again and told them I was going to pretend I was the person who took Snoopy. In my new role I asked them all what they were doing on my land. The child who had told me Snoopy was missing said she had come to get Snoopy. I claimed I didn't know who she was talking about, but played the role with a kindly attitude. The child wasn't deterred, she insisted she wanted Snoopy back. I said if I found Snoopy I'd let them know.

The other members of the group who had been sitting listening to this interaction used what they had heard for the next piece of action. They decided to rescue Snoopy who turned out to be a little girl, but upon investigation they told me that there was a locked metal gate preventing anyone reaching her. I had changed my role back to the park owner and used a low status attitude which, in this case, meant that I was a leader but really didn't know what to do. This left the leadership decisions open to the group. I asked the group what we should do. Someone said the key to the gate was in the bad man's office, and people readily volunteered to go into the office and look for it. The office was the imaginative play area, so we all went to the office and acted out looking for the key with a great deal of tension being added by the threat that the man might return. Just as we had regrouped to consider our next move someone shouted to us that the office was on fire. Lots of different activities took place, some of the group became fire officers, some acted out fetching water and throwing it on the fire and the girl who had told me Snoopy was missing completed the rescue. When all the racing about had stopped she introduced me to the imaginary Snoopy. I said 'Thank goodness you're safe', and we stopped the drama. The session had been almost an hour long.

The children taking part in the lesson I have just described had been in nursery school for one term and already had a grasp of basic groupwork and drama skills. They had demonstrated their ability to listen and to communicate ideas in a variety of ways by talking, drawing and acting out. Notably they spoke to me in a very adult way. They also showed willingness to function as a group for the sake of the story. They had demonstrated naturally acquired learning skills and a positive motivation to learn.

My job as teacher was to keep recreating a framework that would enable any ideas, decisions or actions the children suggested to be used and explored. This provided them with the opportunity to be free to create ideas without having to have a purpose for creating them, without the need for them to have an overview of what they were doing, and without their having to make a critical analysis of their choices and decisions. In my experience any analysis of dramatic action is directly related to the feelings which were generated by it. Sometimes the feelings are obviously gripping, like the excitement of rescuing someone from a cave, and sometimes it is the exciting feeling of creativity which stimulates further thought. With the lesson structure that I have described it was important to value the need to engage with real feelings in the drama, and to understand that this was the first stage of critical analysis.

When pursuing a more explicitly analytical approach, I use clearly defined dramatic conventions as a means of structuring the work.

Conventions such as Freeze Frame, in which a group creates a tableau to represent a significant moment in the story, can serve several purposes. It can define a starting point for the story, for example a Freeze Frame of sharing the last few moments with your family before you set of on a dangerous space adventure. This gives participants in the drama time to think about the context of people working away from their loved ones and make any connections with real life experiences they may have. It can slow action down, so that if there is a disaster in the story such as the space ship crash landing, the participants can recreate the scene with time to discuss the actions and feelings of the whole group in detail. In this example it can also serve as a reflective device, to help consider the problems the people in the story will face as a result of the crash.

The second set of lessons were with a class of Year Five children and focussed on the use of such dramatic conventions as a means of managing learning.

The children's previous experience of drama had mainly been performing assemblies and school plays. I introduced them to classroom drama using two or three lessons of a similar nature to the one I have described above. Gradually, I introduced them to the dramatic conventions by name. They learned what Freeze Frame meant, how to set up Hot-Seating, and how to operate Forum Theatre. My intention was to give them structures which would enable them to create their own frameworks in which to explore their own ideas.

Of course they proved more than capable of making the conventions work. They answered questions about their situation in role with sincerity and sensitivity. They were able to use conventions like Forum Theatre to examine important interactions between people in the science fiction story they had created, and suggest alternative courses of action. For most of the time in these lessons I was working very much like a theatre director. I kept an overview of the story, aware that I was explicitly making a fiction, and I suggested conventions which would challenge the learners to think about the drama deeply and to work towards their own personal interpretation of its meaning.

Following my example, a small group of children in the class developed an understanding of when it was appropriate to use conventions within a drama. The first convention to be selected and used by one of the children was Hot-Seating, which is a way of questioning a person in role. A messenger arrived on the space station without clear identification and the group were suspicious so someone suggested the messenger be Hot-Seated. I supported decisions the class made about how to progress with the drama, and helped to organise the conventions they chose. However, it wasn't very long before the children requested more opportunities to act out scenes uninterrupted by conventions.

I believe the reasons behind this desire to return to spontaneous acting out were located in the learners' understanding of the purpose of doing drama. I am sure that their motivation to do drama came from the excitement of being themselves in a fictional situation. In the fiction they could test out what it was like to be responsible for decisions, and could use their emotional responses to inform their actions without fear of the consequences. With the teacher providing a framework for the action, the drama happened at life pace and seemed more natural and closer to reality. The learners were living through the experience with all the necessary surprises and tensions which made it interesting. They were like a participatory audience, and in this respect they were at a similar stage of understanding to the nursery children. They were not yet interested in using drama to stimulate their thinking in the structured and analytical way that the conventions demanded. What they indicated was the desire to experience a free flow of ideas motivated through feeling.

One lesson that I learned from this was the need to keep a balance between the learners' understanding of the mechanics of making a drama work and their freedom to engage with the drama at an emotional level. For them to use the art form of drama to manage their thinking, there had to be sufficient engagement of their feelings. The conventions could disrupt the flow of the story and lessen the emotional impact which, in turn, seems to lessen motivation. Without motivation the learners have no reason to accept challenges, and further investigation and thinking is lost.

The essential foundation for learner-managed learning in drama is the children's freedom to feel real emotion, and to let those feelings inform the teacher's (and, at a later stage, their own) thinking about the way the work could progress.

In my view the relationship between motivation to learn and feelings is at the core of all issues about how and what people learn. For example, motivation to learn can come from the student's perceived need to conform to teacher in order to gain approval. This is one way in which personal feelings affect learning strategies. In this case, the danger is that learners become dependent on the approval of others to validate their ideas and have little opportunity in their schooling to practise the skills of defining their own real learning needs.

Supporting learner-managed learning requires an understanding of how feelings inform thinking. Learners may use their feelings to make intuitive responses based on what they want at the time. Analysis of the effectiveness of their decisions and actions comes after the experience.

The idea that feelings (positive or negative) are to be valued as central to motivation, raises questions about the structures and teaching strategies used by teachers in all areas of the curriculum, not just in drama. My experience has taught me that some structures get in the way of what learners want, and this can reduce motivation. The key to success is a genuine partnership between teacher and learners that allows real choice about how and what to learn.

*Sharon* is an advisory teacher for drama with Birmingham Education Authority.

# Learner-managed Learning and the Strange Case of Democracy in Action

## *by Roland Meighan*

When there is talk about learner-managed learning, it is frequently about solo learners developing some degree of autonomy in their learning activities. Another approach, however, is that of groups of learners operating as a collective and working as a micro-democracy. The experiences reported here are those of young teacher trainees on courses preparing them for the start of their career in teaching.

The schools of education throughout the country where young people receive their pre-service and in-service training are, by and large, in a sorry state. They tend to be rigid bastions of conventional thinking and practice and highly resistant to change. Actually, the previous two sentences are not mine. They are from the educational psychologist Carl Rogers writing about the situation in the USA. He goes on to say that students in his country have, for the most part, come to regard the courses as a boring waste of time. These comments echo similar things often said about the situation in the UK. This situation is not divorced from the experience of the USA. education system in general, which another writer, E T Hall, suggests has transformed learning from one of the most rewarding of all human activities into a painful, boring, dull, fragmenting, mind-shrinking, soul-shrivelling experience.

Carl Rogers is able to report that he has encountered exceptions where "a human climate for learning is created, where prospective teachers experience the excitement of discovery - both in regard to themselves and the subject matter they will teach. They find it rewarding to be part of a dual process - the process of becoming more of themselves, and the process of promoting and facilitating learning in their students." In the UK the kind of exceptions Rogers describes are mostly to be found in the preparation of Primary school teachers and in particular in some Early Childhood courses.

It is perhaps hard to explain the feeling of relief these comments from the USA bring to me after many years of trying to cope with similar conclusions about teacher education and trying to provide something more effective for prospective teachers against both the authoritarian orthodoxy of the Government QUANGO, The Council for the Accreditation of Teacher Education (CATE), and the continuing practice of most of one's colleagues involved in the preparation of secondary teachers.

The other source of relief has been the positive reaction of the students themselves who can write comments in their course evaluations to the effect that:

> "There was intellectual enjoyment. Intellectual exploration became an exciting and satisfying end in its own right, rather than as a means to a boring and worthless end e.g exams, assessment, the teacher's aims etc."

> "The co-operative spent many hours in discussion and formulated opinions and views (often varying) in relation to our timetable of work. All the group members felt without any reservation whatsoever that the co-op was a new working experience which was stimulating, enjoyable and very worth while."

## Co-operative learning is put on the agenda of possibilities

So, what happens? After a short settling-in period, when the students have introduced each other to the group, the news is broken that although the two tutors, myself and Clive Harber, have a planned course ready in the familiar authoritarian expert style, there are other options open to the group. They can opt for an individualised course based on an individual tutorial system as used at Oxford and Cambridge. This is the solo learner-managed possibility referred to at the outset. They can also consider operating as a democratic learning co-operative that devises and plans its own programme of studies using the tutors as resources if and when deemed appropriate. A specimen contract (see appendix) is available for discussion purposes if this option requires any elaboration.

The course thus begins as a consultation about the methods to be adopted for the course itself. There is in fact another option made available to the group and that is of a mixture of methods e.g. adopting one method for one term and another for another term, or some members choosing an individualised course if the majority want either a lecturer taught course or a learning co-operative.

I perhaps need to clarify what 'a course' actually means. It refers to the Methods of Teaching module of their Post Graduate Certificate of Education year taking up about one third of their total time. These particular students have social studies (economics, politics and sociology) and humanities as their subject goal. The number in the group varied from year to year, from twelve to eighteen.

## Twelve years of experiment

Twelve courses have now been through this initial consultation. In two cases the lecturer taught course was selected for one part of the course and a democratic learning co-operative for another part. One group elected to begin with a taught course for a week or two as a period of familiarisation and then to change to a co-operative approach. The other nine courses have adopted the learning co-operative option from the outset. The learning co-operative experience has been externally monitored twice, once by an independent university evaluator and once during a visitation by a team of Her Majesty's Inspectors.

The tutors had to adjust to a different theory of teaching and so did most of the students. Both tutors and most of the students had been educated in one or other of the authoritarian styles where the majority of the decisions had been made for them rather than by them and therefore they were used to being either the anvil or the hammer. The tutors had to learn:

- to listen much more than they had been used to, and learn to resist their previous habits of dominating the decision making.

- to cope with the anxiety aroused when their expertise was seen to be less significant than they had previously supposed.

- to trust the learners to apply their intelligence in planning and executing a course. This was against all the previous training of both students and tutors and in opposition to the strongly held beliefs of most colleagues.

- to cope with the anxiety of sharing power. There was considerable irony in feeling anxious at having helped students to manage competently on their own when this is exactly what they would need to do for the duration of their careers. Were we really earning our money by facilitation rather than instruction?

- to cope with the tasks of facilitation which proved to be demanding in identifying sources, making contacts, and solving operational problems on the spot or at short notice: this helped satisfy our Protestant Work Ethic habituations. The easier authoritarian option of preparing handouts and resources well in advance suddenly seemed very comfortable, safe and strangely appealing.

- the tutors also had to cope with their ideas and suggestions being scrutinised closely, with justification being requested and sometimes rejected as inappropriate. They had to learn the difficult lesson of humility. They had to learn the significance of the saying:

> *"Of a good leader, when his task is finished, his goal achieved, they say, 'We did this ourselves'."* **Lao-tse c.600 B.C.**

The students had to make considerable adjustments too. These included the following:

- to redefine preparation for teaching as active rather than passive: to accept the idea that since teaching was primarily a decision making activity, the way to learn might be to simulate the process using themselves as guinea pigs by selecting the aims, content, methods, and evaluations for their own learning. Previous experience had an influence here:

> *"We all felt that the work that we had been engaged upon for our first degree courses had been too competitive and too isolated. Therefore we all agreed that something else had to be attempted for our year within the faculty."*

- to take responsibility for their own and others' learning. This was seen as improving standards in contrast to the predictions of colleagues that students would not devise the 'best' course:

> *"With all students choosing the range of subjects, the content, inevitably (in my mind) was of a greater range and of more relevance than if the 'teacher' had done all the choosing. A group of students, especially from different specialist backgrounds, was able to provide more resources that one teacher could."*

- to acquire both techniques for survival in schools as they were, alongside a vision for future educational possibilities:

> *"The course, in practice, seemed to me to cope nicely with the idealism of educational change and the practicalities and constraints involved in operationalising such changes. In this way the course provided a realistic 'vision' for changed procedures in teaching whilst not ignoring the problems of practice, or survival, which face all teachers."*

- to cope with the realisation that they were able to motivate themselves:

> *"I felt great responsibility for the course and this involvement meant always taking a mentally active part. I felt no resentment against somebody trying to impose work or a situation on me.*

*Thus motivation was high."*

## Solo and collective learner-managed learning in partnership

The stress in this account has been on the collective aspect of the learning. In reality, the courses required the development of both the solo type of learner-managed and the collective form, in interaction with each other. The group used the device of allocating tasks to individuals, and sometimes pairs and trios, which required them to go off and research and prepare material, activities and sessions. The results of their solo activities would then be fed back into the group programme.

## Better or worse teachers?

Initially there was apprehension about how students involved in a democratic learning co-operative would fare on teaching practice, with job applications and with interviews. Such apprehension is now a thing of the past. Students used to making decisions about what to learn, assembling appropriate materials and using them with a selected method and then evaluating the outcome, tend to transfer these behaviours to the school situation with some confidence. And being used to working co-operatively, they fitted into team situations with relative ease.

The feedback from applications for posts and interviews has also denied the early apprehension. The approach of the students seems to appeal to many interviewers. Head teachers have been known to phone the tutors with comments like "this is a whole new generation of prospective teachers, articulate, enthusiastic, industrious, and challenging."

## Towards giving prospective teachers curiosity, courage, confidence and criticism

In contrast to the remarks of Hall quoted earlier about learning being turned into a mind-shrinking and soul-shrivling experience, James Hemming, an independent and eminent educational psychologist, has argued that some of the key characteristics of successful education are the three C's of curiosity, courage and confidence to which he adds a fourth, that of criticism in the sense of self-evaluation. The approach, through offering the experience of learning co-operatives to prospective teachers, has encouraged me to see this as a step in the direction of such achievements. It would be foolish, however, to overstate the claims. The writer is all too aware of the observations about the limitations of democratic approaches:

> *"Democracy is the worst system of organisation -- except for all the others."* **Winston Churchill**

> *"So, two cheers for democracy: one because it admits variety and two because it permits criticism. Two cheers are quite enough: there is no occasion to give three."* **E M Forster**

(Fuller accounts of the courses described above are in print and can be obtained from the author.)

## Appendix

### Group Learning Contract

We agree to accept responsibility for our course as a group.

We agree to take an active part in the learning of the group.

We agree to be constructively critical of our own and other people's ideas.

We agree to plan our own programme of studies, implement it using the group members and appointed teachers as resources, and review the outcomes in order that we may learn from any limitations we identify. We agree to the keeping of a group log-book of work completed, planning decisions, session papers and any other appropriate documents.

We agree to share the duties of being in the chair, the task of being meeting secretary and the roles of session organisers and contributors.

We agree to review this contract from time to time.

### References

Chamberlin, R (1989) *Free Children and Democratic Schools* (London, Falmer)

Engle, S and Ochoa, A (1989) *Education for Democratic Citizenship* (Columbia, Teachers College Press)

Gordon, T (1986) *Democracy in one School?* (London, Falmer) Harber, C and Meighan, R, (1989) *The Democratic School: Educational Management and the Practice of Democracy.* (Ticknall, Education Now

Books)

Meighan, R (1986) *A Sociology of Educating* (second edition) (London, Cassell)

Meighan, R (1988) *Flexischooling* (Ticknall, Education Now Books)

Rogers, C (1983) *Freedom to Learn for the Eighties* (Colombus, Ohio, Merrill)

Nicholls, J. G (1989) *The Competitive Ethos and Democratic Education* (Cambridge Massechusetts, Harvard Univ. Press)

White, P (1983) *Beyond Domination,* (London, Routledge and Kegan Paul)


Roland is Senior Lecturer in Education at the University of Birmingham.

# The Hijack of Young Children's Learning.
*by Janet Meighan*

It is with concern, then frustration, then helplessness, that parents and educators of young children have noted that their curiosity, confidence and enthusiasm for learning evaporate. In addition, the key element of personal management of their activities, so frequently changes to one of passive dependence as they grow older and pass through our educational system. Learning how to learn gives way to learning how to be taught. The lost opportunities for learning and personal development are only too apparent as we witness the large numbers of teenagers and adults who resist the idea of continuing education yet appear to be failing in achieving personal satisfaction in their lives.

As the demand grows for an adult population able to contribute to the challenges of a developing modern society, and at the same time achieve greater personal fulfilment, it is essential that individuals are equipped for this challenge. To have some stake in a constantly changing society involves some degree of personal participation, initiative, responsibility and critical appraisal. Our present educational system is sadly failing to support and extend personal development of this nature. Paradoxically, these characteristics are very evident in the confident learning behaviour of young children.

So frequently, the processes engaged in by young children during their learning are taken for granted. When observing infants attempting to grasp a desired object which is almost out of reach, we recognise the effort, stimulated by curiosity and self-motivation, that is made. There is learning by repeated trial and error; self-reliance in solving simple problems by attempting new tactics when the first ones fail; the self-directed sequencing of movements. Only if all autonomous attempts fail do we hear the call for the help of others!

## Play is children's work

The play of young children has been widely researched and many generalisations made about its contribution to learning. But it is perhaps in the opportunities it presents for exploration and concrete, first hand experiences that we find evidence of self-directed activity and observe situations where the child has some control.

Young children familiarizing themselves with a new toy or object prior to playing with it, engage in what Corinne Hutt (1982) identified as 'exploratory play'; a preliminary stage to playing as first the child attempts to learn something about the toy or object - what it looks like, how it feels, what can be done with it - learning from first hand exploration. When some degree of familiarity, mastery and confidence is achieved, the child is able to move to the stage of playing that involves working towards a self-determined goal. For example, Susan aged four having explored and mastered the possibilities of an assortment of wooden blocks, decided to build a garage for her new toy car. The self-directed activity involved her in some simple planning, imagining based on past experience, decision making and problem solving in the positioning of the blocks, plus dealing with frustration when the roof caved in.

John Holt's close observations of young children, as reported in books such as 'Learning All the Time', yield the same conclusion about the quality of their learning. He proposes that children are " .... acting like scientists all the time, which is to say looking, noticing, wondering, theorizing, testing their theories, and changing them as often as they have to."

When young children's imaginative play involves the adoption of roles, as in the creation of a cafe situation, we may see imitative play resulting from observation of and reflection on adult models. We may also witness fantasy play as new experiences are developed, providing opportunities for the organisation of ideas and the development of complex, abstract, divergent thinking. This example of play may be a solitary activity, as is frequently the case with very young children, or co-operative. Working with others, whether they are peer group or adults, presents other challenges for the self-governing learner. "Do I accept the ideas, the help, the advice they offer?". "If so, how will they affect my ideas, my plans?". Language increasingly becomes an important element in communication and in the reasoning necessary for personal management of experiences.

## Adults as learning 'coaches' or learning 'hijackers'?

The contribution of adults to the young child's skills in the management of their learning is increasingly debated. Kathy Sylva, among others, points to the value of an adult 'partner' in play experiences. The need for their support and encouragement in the confidence building process is evident, but John Holt gives two warnings about too much interference and uninvited teaching:

" .... interfering very much in the play and learning of children often stops it altogether."

"Not only is it the case that uninvited teaching does not make learning, but - and this was even harder for me to learn - for the most part such teaching prevents learning."

Steve, aged three, investigating an old, but still working typewriter which had been given to him, made full use of his parents by asking "What's that?", "Why?" in his early explorations, before moving to the stage of independent activity and learning. He only asked for help when his own problem solving strategies failed, and even then he learnt that it was not always immediately available! Perhaps the view of the adult as 'learning coach' is an appropriate analogy.

There is much evidence of opportunities for self-directed learning in many good nursery schools and classes in this country, but the ideas developed in the Ypsilanti, Michigan, Pre-school Project (Weikart et al 1978) at the High/Scope Foundation present a particularly useful model for the development of skills in learner-managed learning which may be modified to fit a range of settings and ages. Quite simply this can be expressed as 'Plan - Do - Review'. At the High/Scope Foundation children as young as three were encouraged to plan their activities, with the support of an adult, which involved consideration of the decisions which needed to be made. The implementation of the planning involved perseverance to see it through, as well as opportunities to develop both a range of skills and the ownership of subsequent knowledge. The process of reviewing the activity on its completion with both an adult and peers, encouraged reflection and even justification for courses of action taken. Greater detail is provided by Gill Payne (1989) in 'Plan-Do-Review .... an active approach to children's learning.' (Also Weikart et al 1978). Although the plan-do-review approach as developed in Ypsilanti required a high adult:child ratio, and was structured to encourage the development of skills in decision making and evaluation, many nursery and infant teachers in this country have incorporated the fundamental ideas into their own practice of enabling young children to develop some autonomy in their learning.

It is no surprise, therefore, that these teachers together with parents are concerned, frustrated and helpless when the young learners, who have been developing autonomy, appear to be subjected to a hijack in the dubious cause of substituting dependence in the form of 'learning how to be taught' for the independence of 'learning how to learn'.

## Reading and references

Hutt, C (1982) *Exploration and play in children*.

Herron, R E and Sutton-Smith, B (Eds) *Child's Play* (New York, John Wiley)

Moyles, J R (1989) *Just Playing? The Role and Status of Play in Early Childhood Education* (Open University Press)

Payne, G (1989) *Plan-Do-Review...an active approach to children's learning*.

Meighan, J (Ed) *Early Years Education: Education for being* Education Now No.5, 1989.

Sylva, K Roy, C and Painter, M (1980) *Child Watching at Playgroup and Nursery School* (London, Grant McIntyre)

Weikart, D P, Epstein, A S, Schweinhart, L, Bond, J T (1978) *The Ypsilanti Pre-school Curriculum Demonstration Project: Pre-school Years and Longitudinal Results* (Ypsilanti, Michigan, High/Scope Educational Research Foundation)

Janet is Honorary Senior Lecturer in Education at Derby College of Higher Education.

## "I Want to Learn!"

## Learner-managed learning in the early years of school

*by Sue Hannath*

When children come into our schools at the age of four and a half, they have already acquired a vast amount of knowledge. They have learned to communicate with the world, both verbally and physically, and the majority of these skills have been acquired by the child *wanting* to learn. From the earliest age young children take ownership of what they are doing. They may include others, peers or adults, or they may work in isolation. An adult can offer help and guidance and can 'teach' a child if she is ready to take on board whatever skill is being encouraged. Young children are like sponges - they soak up information. They are enquiring, questioning and interested and, through these processes, they are able to make informed decisions.

It is with all of these skills that a child comes to the formal setting of a school. In partnership with parents, the school can encourage and develop these skills and can extend the learning process the children have already begun. Or it can start to rely on a different authoritarian approach where children attend school 'to be taught' and 'to learn'! Learner-managed learning can be continued and developed, or substituted for learning to have learning managed by someone else.

Children also arrive at school with very positive attitudes towards themselves and the things they can and cannot do. They understand that skills are developed, and that they will achieve new skills through the passage of time. Many times I have heard children say 'When I'm grown up I will be able to .... ' do whatever they aspire to. They have not experienced failure in terms of negative responses, only as new and difficult challenges. They understand that they have not yet reached a stage in their own development to achieve all their aspirations.

In my classroom I fight long and hard to ensure that all children's needs are met and that I encourage the processes of learning rather than switching children off. I encourage children to take ownership of their education, making them aware of possibilities by open-ended questioning. For example, if the children are designing vehicles to see which will travel furthest down a ramp, I might ask: 'What kind of materials are you going to use?', 'How can you attach the wheels?', 'What makes the best kind of wheels?', 'Can you make the vehicle go faster or in a straight line?', 'Does the shape of the vehicle make a difference? If so, why?'. My questions are always of the what?, how?, tell me, can you?, why? type - the very questions children bombard adults with from the day they start talking.

My room is organised so as to provide the wealth of resources necessary to maintain the children's curiosity and develop their enquiring minds. For example, there is a comfortable, inviting book corner with carpets, cushions, bean bags and chairs where books of various kinds and story tapes are immediately accessible at any time of day. Computers are also available at all times, switched on ready, with software suitable for children at all levels of development nearby. Even the youngest child can load a programme and feel confident enough to have a go without adult intervention and interruption.

The imaginative play area is more than a 'home corner'. Changed regularly, it is a place where anything can happen: a boat sailing away to where the wild things are, or a space rocket exploring the moon, for instance. The possibilities for imaginative play are endless.

I believe that learner-managed learning will continue to grow only if the environment of the school is warm, friendly, stimulating and organised in such a way that children can select and discover approriate materials for the task in hand. In my room all the equipment is readily accessible: glue, scissors, paper, card, pencils, crayons, paints, felt tips, rulers, calculators, maths equipment - all clearly labelled and stored where children know they will always find them, and where they must always put them back! Dusters, dustpans, brushes and cloths are also to hand, the children being responsible for all their actions, including the spillages and messes. Collections of materials in the classroom are a huge resource - the children can compare, select and reject in order to accomplish whatever task they're working on.

I help children develop their autonomy by making these resources available, and by devising strategies so that they can have a go at whatever the challenge is and develop reasoned questioning in order to help themselves. If children are permanently taught in an authoritarian way, where everything is tightly structured and directed, with precise instructions and a pre-determined end result, then their own curiosity and personal development becomes restricted and they are only fulfilling the teacher's expectations. Authoritarian styles have a modest part to play in the scheme of things provided they are used sparingly, and sensitively as Janet Meighan, quoting John Holt, indicates in the previous article.

The children in our school are learners, not passive receivers of information. They take an active role. For example, in an activity where children are going to record, they need to look at a wide range of possibilities: a factual account, a cartoon illustration, a description, a pure illustration, a collage, a model, a mobile. Then they will be able to decide for themselves the best way to present their work without being bound by what the teacher decides is acceptable.

In order to meet the requirements imposed by law in the Education Reform Act and embodied in the National Curriculum, teachers need to use a variety of organisational strategies, whole class teaching, group work and individual teaching, to fulfull their obligations. However, unless children are encouraged to take ownership and develop their own ideas and questions, their education will be limited to producing an output restricted to teacher input rather than developing the motivation to explore further. The National Curriculum has given us a basic framework to work with, but the way we implement it is still in the hands of teachers and parents, working in partnership. I shall still try to work on the assumption that confidence and trust in the children must underpin all that we do in school.

Assessment, for example, is a crucial area. By taking the opportunity to explore at first hand, to reflect upon the work they have achieved and to discuss their thoughts openly with receptive adults, children are able to assess their progress for themselves, rather than be the recipients of someone else's opinion.

As a profession we are always able to implement the process of learning in a flexible way, if we so choose, in order to encourage independence and help all children to sustain the desire to learn throughout their lifetimes, to continue to 'want to learn'.

*Sue* is Deputy Headteacher at a Derbyshire primary school.

## Teaching Learners to Manage
*by Paul Ginnis*

This odd, apparently self-contradictory title is designed to spotlight the attitudes and behaviours of teachers who are serious about enabling learners to learn autonomously. At the heart of the approach is the concept of personal responsibility, a tough one to grasp .... and to practice.

Recently, I talked with a technology teacher who was looking for advice on Year 9 students' motivation. He wanted them to be excited about the planning and design phase of their work and was upset that his customary practice of giving the class a topic, asking them to brainstorm individually (!), then in pairs, and come up with a problem to invent solutions about .... wasn't grabbing the kids. He believed that he was 'giving the children ownership of their work'. Why weren't they taking it?

This process, which in one form or another is common in schools, simply asked students to have ideas about someone else's idea, to paint in the details, as it were, on a canvas designed by the master. A crucial decision had already been made -- that the topic would be 'Entertainment' - which the teacher thought was sufficiently broad and open-ended. The children, however, still behaved as if they were being made to work.

Imagine what would have happened if the teacher had started with these questions instead: 'What interests you about technology?' or 'In what ways do you want technology to be of use to you?' or 'What can you already do in this subject and what would you like to be able to do?' or 'What reasons do you have for doing technology at this stage? Does it meet any of your interests or needs at the moment?'

Actually, most teachers I know wouldn't have wanted to start like this because they, like most parents, operate on the premise that it's their job to take responsibility for children. How many of them would let the students' answers to the basic questions above determine their learning? 'But they might not want to learn anything! They might want to learn something they don't need to know, and not learn something vital.'

Yes, they might. They would then be managing their learning. I am suggesting that the minimum for a teacher or parent who wants to operate learner-managed learning is to *trust the learner.* This deep feeling within the teacher is the basis of the facilitating relationship. Carl Rogers goes on: "the facilitation of significant learning rests upon certain attitudinal qualities that exist in the relationship between the facilitator and the learner." (1) Specific ways of behaving and intervening then follow, and although these can be learned I have found that they don't work for teachers who don't have the basic orientation, and they tend to come naturally to those who do. At one stage, after many years experience and research, Rogers identified three such attitudes (2). In my work as a teacher and advisory teacher I have noticed, and recommend to you, the kinds of behaviours which relate to them.

**Realness**

First, is 'realness is the facilitator of learning'. This refers to the teacher being herself, a real person with the children, not wearing a mask or playing a role as most teachers do. It means being obviously unsure at times, displaying feelings and talking openly about them, being honest about beliefs, worries and excitements .... having fun as well as being serious and sharing some information about personal life. All these would be natural steps in forming a friendship. The children using the teacher's first name is another indication of her willingness to be a person with them.

The key is for the teacher to tell the truth, the whole truth and nothing but the truth. In other words, letting the children in on what she is thinking and feeling. For example, instead of 'We need to move to another room', she might say 'I feel it's too noisy in here, and as we've already got all our stuff out I'm not sure what to do?' This leads to another important habit: ask the learners, whenever a dilemma or question comes to mind.

Another aspect of telling the truth is to be clear with students about the bottom lines. All teachers and parents have limits on acceptable behaviour and standards of one sort or another. It's best for everyone if these limits are made known, so that teachers don't feel compromised and learners don't feel conned.

Modelling mistakes. Accepting new challeges and taking risks usually involves making mistakes. It is important for students to see this as a natural part of the learning process .... for adults too. It is tempting for teachers disguise their mistakes. It is more helpful to be honest about them and exemplify a way of handling them positively.

Now add to this list anything else that would avoid distance between teacher and learner: sitting down with students; removing physical barriers like desks; dressing informally ....

### Empathetic Understanding

Another of Roger's key qualities is 'empathetic understanding'. "When the teacher has the ability to understand the student's reactions from the inside, has a sensitive awareness of the way the process of education and learning seems to the student, then again the likelihood of significant learning is increased." (3) The students can be asked about their feelings regularly. For example, 'What are your priorities for the coming term?', 'What do you feel is the best way forward from here?', 'How do you feel about the way things are going at the moment?'

Teachers are often afraid of students' negative feelings, such as boredom. Rather than pretend or insist that the boredom doesn't exist, the teacher can acknowledge the feeling ('I understand that you are bored') and go on to ask 'What would it take for you to be more interested in the work?' or 'Would you like to carry on what you're doing or do something else now and come back to this later?' Once acknowledged, negative feelings tend to disappear anyway, if ignored they tend to harden. All the time the teacher regards the learner as responsible for herself, so will ask her to create and make choices for herself. It's tempting instead for the teacher to start taking responsibility for the student: 'I think you could .... ', 'Why don't you .... '. It's important to know the difference between support and rescue; to do the former and resist the latter.

So, asking appropriate questions, not leading ones but open ones, is a way of prompting the student to be responsible for herself. Above all, the teacher needs to listen actively, feeding back to students what they are saying, without interpretation or opinion, so they know they are heard and understood, and left with the (sometimes painful) responsibility for choices.

### Unconditional Positive Regard

The third attitude is 'prizing, acceptance, trust' which elsewhere Rogers calls 'unconditional positive regard'. Many teachers operate a system of conditional regard instead. Their behaviours say to students

'I will like you if you .... or when you .... '. Giving house points, letting those who are sitting up straight go first, smiling at some, scowling at others, giving smiley faces and sweets for good work, phrases like 'Good girl', 'I'm proud of you', 'I'm ashamed of you', sending people out of the room, being disgusted and shocked, speaking sarcastically .... are just some of the ways in which teachers signal their approval or disapproval of students.

No-one likes to be disapproved of, and the drive to be accepted is so strong that it plays directly into the hands of adults, giving them a cheap way of controlling behaviour. All they have to do is make clear which behaviours gain approval and they lead the children into a complex world of manipulative 'games playing' where personal autonomy is innocently surrendered. The door is then open to widespread damage as learners come to depend on the mechanism.

In the learner-managed approach there is no room for routines which smack of approval-disapproval, or indeed anything which attempts to manipulate students and keep them dependent on external factors. So, we say goodbye to rewards and punishments of all kinds, to prizegiving, to merit marks, star charts, prefects, monitors, competitive learning and to forms of assessment which make comparisons. In their place is "a prizing of the learner as an imperfect human being with many feelings, many potentialities." (4)

Punishment will be replaced by skilled counselling which asks the student to take responsibility for his actions and their consequences. Making contracts is a positive way of strengthening students' own behavioural or learning intentions. Students are heard, their views and feelings are accepted as they are without being interpreted, censored or judged. Praise is replaced by acknowledgement and positive feedback. Compare 'Well done, you did a good job' with 'I appreciate you finishing that, thank you'. Likewise, criticism is replaced by negative feedback. For example, 'You're too slow. That should have been done in half the time' could be replaced with 'I noticed how long you took to do that. There are quicker ways of doing it which I am willing to show you if you want.' With honest feedback in place, rigorous self-assessment can be relied on.

Being caught in the approval-disapproval net creates high levels of anxiety: 'I must I get it right.' The natural consequence of this for the student is to play safe, to go for what she knows she will succeed at. Risk-taking is then at a minimum. To untangle this, teachers can find ways of avoiding right and wrong, by encouraging investigations and discoveries and by prompting students to check their findings, or try and prove them, so that being 'wrong' is turned back into learning and is not 'bad'.

The teacher constantly lets the learner know that her standing in the teacher's eyes is not in jeopardy, that positive regard given one minute will not be withdrawn the next. If the student's behaviour is unacceptable, then the teacher can say so and be firm about it, without seeming to reject the person because of it. Loving the sinner while hating the sin is a good old Augustinian concept.

The deepest and most permanent damage done by approval-disapproval is to self-esteem. People easily get to the point where they like themselves only inasmuch as they are liked by others. They go out of their way to present themselves as likeable, lovable or praiseworthy in order to receive positive strokes. Behaviour is contorted to match the known, or suspected, attitudes of the audience. Children and adults regularly deny themselves what they really want, sometimes to the point of grotesque self-sacrifice, and will do the very things they hate .... all because the approval of others matters most. Such people are not free to learn, they subject themselves to a subtle and pernicious form of extrinsic control. The only antidote to this is strong self-esteem which, in turn, is created by consistently experiencing unconditional positive regard.

## Challenging teaching

So, the teacher is challenged on two fronts: to enhance students' self-esteem while the tentacles of approval-disapproval seem to reach into every area of life - family, friendships, schooling, employment; and to raise students' sense of self-responsibility whereas the world we live in is geared to people blaming others, to scapegoating, getting-away-with-it-if-you-can, looking for excuses ....

In turn, the teacher may need to challenge the students. One way of doing this is to use the language of personal responsibility consistently and require students to do the same. For example, begin sentences with 'I' rather than 'You', 'They' or 'One'. This encourages the speaker to own their feelings and thoughts. For example, change 'You make me feel' to 'I feel'; change 'This always happens to me' to 'I do this a lot'. Avoid the word 'try' as it can provide a cop-out and weaken intention. Also avoid asking people 'why' as this creates defensiveness and presses people to explain their behaviour away. Change 'can't' to 'won't' in sentences like 'I can't settle down to my work.' Change 'but' to 'and', for example 'I want to get my work finished, but I haven't got time'. Avoid using 'should', 'must', 'ought' and any other moralising statement which attempts to put people under obligation.

Another strategy is to ask students to drop old ideas about themselves. People often play 'old tapes' such as 'I'm no good at Maths' or 'I can't sing'. Ask them instead to say 'I've found Maths difficult up to now', 'I used to think I could never sing.' These tapes are largely the result of labelling by adults, for example through sweeping 'You are. .... /You are not .... ' statements, through streaming and setting, through crass assessments and so on. Such judgemental and discriminatory practices are the antithesis of unconditional positive regard.

Learners are almost always part of a group, large or small. This, I believe, is desirable and provides a microcosm in which the norms of our society can be replaced. The teacher can challenge the group to exemplify the conditions which support self-esteem and self-responsibility. Ground rules can be negotiated which everyone is responsible for keeping and monitoring. Put downs, in any form, can be banned. Listening skills can be taught to the group, so can assertiveness. A circle can become the accepted structure for group interaction, promoting openness and listening.

Learner-managed learning doesn't just happen by teachers throwing out 'ownership' as the technology teacher did. It requires the teacher to demonstrate specific attitudes, exemplified by specific behaviours, consistently. In time, students may come to trust themselves, the process and the teacher enough to fly solo. At this point there will be genuine motivation for self-management, then the coaxing, the carrying and the conning can stop.

## References

1. Rogers, C (1983) 'The Interpersonal Relationship in the Facilitation of Learning' *Freedom to Learn for the Eighties* (Columbus, Ohio, Merrill) p.121
2. *op cit* 3. op cit p 125
4. op cit p 124

# Studies in Independence

## Learner-managed learning at Dame Catherine's School, Ticknall

*by Philip Toogood*

Dame Catherine's School in the tiny South Derbyshire village of Ticknall has been going for nearly five years. In itself it is an affirmation of the confidence of the parents that they can set up and run a school, employ teachers to teach, raise the money without charging fees, manage the Catherine Wheel Shop, manage the material side of the school, clean and maintain the buildings and garden, help with the teaching when possible and desirable .... and still have some time for their personal lives!

Dame Catherine's is a study in independence. It is effectively a cry from our culture of silence which has made it necessary in this country to go along with things as they are, to consign one's children to the local maintained school or to pay through the nose to go private.

It is a challenging invitation to a third way, of autonomy with support. At present Dame Catherine's has the autonomy of independence from the State system and some support from charitable funds to eke out what the parent-run shop can make (a remarkable 1/3 of the annual budget!). One day, perhaps, Dame Catherine's will have the support of the public purse without any loss of autonomy.

It would be strange therefore if the daily education of the children ignored that most pressing problem of our times: how to learn to think for oneself and to assert the truth by standing out for what is right and responsible in the world of today.

Independent studies ought to lead directly to self-realisation by the learner. The essence of this, as we see it at Dame Catherine's, is in learning how to learn rather than in learning how to be taught. Nowhere has this been better expressed than in the writing of the Brazilian educator of the urban poor, Paolo Freire. He writes of a 'praxis' in the process of learning.

The first movement in this praxis is the 'conscientization' of the learner. The learner must become deeply aware of the problem which confronts. The learner is thus motivated to reflect on the nature of the problem, using all the skills of rational perception. Conclusions are then articulated clearly and refined carefully. Action follows. Problems experienced in the action are reviewed and the whole cycle is repeated. This is the process of PLAN-DO-REVIEW.

Plan-do-review learning is necessarily social. It requires the active participation of other people. It requires these people to be co-learners, taking part in the development of critical awareness. It should be distinguished from individual learning. It is this critical awareness developed in the young people of today which provides the hope for a better world tomorrow. Without it there is little hope that the pressing problems will begin to be addressed, let alone solved.

Freire asserted that the process of learning how to learn, which embodies this theory of 'praxis', requires the teacher to intervene in the process itself. The learner will come to the learning with a range of misconceptions, or at least of conceptions which should be put to the test of challenge and refinement. The style of intervention by the teacher will have to be varied across a spectrum of intervention styles, from the facilitative to the authoritative. At times the teacher will actually be a learner alongside the student. At others she will be instructing, facilitating, managing resources, evaluating and involving the student in self-evaluation. Plan-do-review should be paralleled by Can-do in the attitude of the teacher towards the tasks or problems confronting the learner. Above all, the teacher should be more than taskmaster. Independent studies should lead to a practice of self-set tasks where the learner becomes the taskmaster.

At Dame Catherine's we realised early that the small groups we were with all day presented a particular opportunity and a special pitfall which we have tried to avoid. The particular opportunity was that whatever we did we were likely to appear to succeed. The small group nature of the school, the parental concern and support, the beautiful country environment .... all led in this direction. The pitfall was that whichever style of teaching we adopted this was likely to be so for the majority of children. They would become extremely good at being taught, if we were not very careful.

It became a matter of prime importance that Freire's praxis: conscientization (the development of awareness), reflection, articulation and action should be built into the daily practice of learning. The school has three sections: Reception/Infant to 7 years old; Junior from 7 to 11 years old; and Secondary from 11 to 16 years. This resolve to teach so as to learn how to learn is present in all three sections.

What is common to all three is the emphasis given in the organisation of time and space to meeting in small circles .... an echo, perhaps, of Freire's own study circles by which means he attempted (very successfully) to spread literacy amongst the oppressed peasantry of Brazil. Our days begin in small circles, which are frequently returned to, and sessions are often ended in this way.

At the whole school weekly meeting we try to get as perfect a circle as possible and no child or teacher is allowed to sit out. The teacher, student or visitor who arrives after the meeting has started has to find a chair and sit in the circle enlarged for the purpose of involving them. Eye contact, face to face assertions, can only be made in this way. The meetings proceed usually without a prepared reading or talk or 'performance' because we feel that this might interrupt the process of actually meeting, of being together and giving expression to what we want to say. There is no intention to derive decisions or official outcomes. It is a time to dwell on our mutual concerns. It is very surprising how this often works out. Children are frequently bursting to say something which may lead on to a theme being developed or it may not. Sometimes children want to recite something, or read something, maybe just tell a story or make an observation. It is a time to develop the art of conversation, observing the listening passages, the right moment to join in, to change the subject or develop a theme, to laugh, be alarmed, mourn, celebrate or simply keep quiet, inward thought.

These meetings in circles, continued at the simple lunches which we sit down for and which are preceded by someone volunteering a word of thankfulness for the food, begin the process of 'conscientisation', or of 'becoming aware', without which much of our learning would be meaningless, however successfully externally imposed criteria for the learning may have been met.

In the Secondary section, although we do have a Time Frame for each half term, week and day, the days are often re-planned at our short circle meetings. Even the Time Frame is the subject of a meeting at the end of each half term and students offer suggestions for new activities or for changes in the existing plan. In this way a sense of the ownership of the daily experience is begun. A motivation to carry things through is arrived at.

We are moving towards a formalisation of this process in the Secondary section whereby the whole of the curriculum is planned with the small group in a series of 'Learning Experience Activity

Packages' (LEAPS, as the American City As School pioneers called them).

I gave some thought to these LEAPS with the first Secondary section I had at Dame Catherine's and we worked out a format for them:
- the student develops a self-portrait (Who am I ?);
- a stage of writing what they want to do in the forthcoming half term, what I want them to do and what is the common understanding of what they ought to be doing at this time in their lives (What can I do?);
- thence into a plan for what they are going to do, to be validated by all three parties, the student, parent and teacher (What I am going to do!);
- finally to a portfolio of comments, records, and evidence of what had actually been done, and hence 'achieved' in the sense that it had to be 'accredited' or celebrated in some more or less formal way. (What I have done!).

The idea was that this portfolio should be displayed for trusted adults to come and see and talk over with the student in a manner so as to express understanding and appreciation of the work done. Of course, formal certification was possible through external assessment in exams as well at this stage. The idea was that this should all lead to a restarting of the process so that what had been achieved was fed into the next stage of 'Who am I?'

As we move towards a full blown Flexi College in Derby we are once again setting out on the process of making LEAPS.

The Infant/Reception and Junior sections also consciously engage in Independent Studies and in the Juniors every day starts off with an Independent Studies time after a short group meeting in a circle. Crucial to these sessions is the design of the classroom, the time given to the activity, the disposition of the resources, the way the tutor works and the planning and assessment with the students which goes on continuously. In other words the five main variables of any planned learning situation are carefully taken into account: Territory, Time, Teacher(s), Things and the Thinking before, during and after.

It is deliberate, for example, that Independent Studies takes place *first thing every day.* If a student comes in and discusses what is to be done and then does it I reckon there is more chance of 'conscientization', reflection, articulation and action taking place, than if the first thing which happens is that the teacher leads off with an introduction.

There is time for more direct teacher-led small group sessions after the 'tone' for the daily work-song has been sounded in Independent Studies. Similarly, following a quiet reading session after lunch, the days end with Activity sessions of dance, drama, music, art, swimming, sport, and so on. Thus each day reflects the praxis of Freire.

It is deliberate also that the classroom of the Juniors is set out in a particular way. It was the result, in the Christmasmas 1990 break of some 132 person-hours of work between myself, a team of parents and a visiting Polish architecture student who was going blind! Together we made the personal study units round 2 sides of the classroom, made the little craft area, the display units, the discussion space, the central group tables, the art area, library area and computer space. Now when the parents come in to clean on a rota after school it is possible to point out the whys and wherefores of this arrangement to the newcomers and to discuss how it is working.

These Independent Studies sessions are not confined to reading, writing, book investigation, Maths work cards and so on. I know directly of this because the Juniors' tutor, Sarah Woodfield, takes my secondary group for Life Science once a week while I tutor her Independent Studies session.

The children seem to have so many interesting things to do, from going out into the garden to tend their vegetable or flower plots, to drawing, painting, making, writing stories, working in pairs or small groups preparing drama, poetry, talks, investigating, doing programmed work, doing surveys or simply reading. I notice also, and approve, the inclusion of rote learning of favourite poems, of tables, spellings and so on, matters which indicate that in the creative atmosphere of dialogue in our small school we are fully aware that there are many ways of learning and that it is stultifying to limit it to only one.

From the moment the tiny child sets foot inside Dame Catherine's, possibly to play while the mother or father does cleaning duty after school, thereby coming into contact with those who are gradually dispersing, there is a process at work of growing assertiveness. It is not a question of precocious self-centredness (in fact boundaries to behaviour are continuously placed and moved by adults and by older and younger children), but more a question of growing self-confidence acquired in an atmosphere of mutual respect and hard work. There is an attempt at Dame Catherine's to spread the sense that whatever is happening is the most important thing that could be happening and that it is important in itself rather than for what it might lead to.

An example of this is the way that the Infants join in the planning, action and review of their work in literature, art and drama. This sets a vibrant real-life context for their attempts to learn to read and to understand, to write, to explain and to make their own creations. This growing assertiveness is a manifestation of self- and other- identification. It leads, and can be seen to lead, to deep and lasting developments in their personalities, in their value systems, in their aspirations and in the transformation of themselves into people who stand a chance of becoming more critically aware and therefore likely to be of more use to themselves and to others in their lives.

It is this quality of independence, or of autonomy or self-determination in their studies which lies at the heart of 'real learning'. In other circumstances independent learning can become simply individual learning, students following a pre-set programmed course on their own, or exploring, without that critical self- and other- awareness, matters which lead to the acquisition of a certain sort of false confidence.

In all of this the teacher has an important part to play as a sort of reflective agent in the student's learning. The teacher who uses didactic teaching, who sets off the explorations and stands back to come in at the end as a judge, parodies the essential privilege which a teacher has, of being that unobtrusive but insistent presence, a sort of 'secret sharer', often unacknowledged, who sticks in with the process of developing awareness until no longer required.

*Philip* is Head of Dame Catherine's School.

# Principles, Possibilities and Problems

## Learner-managed learning and libertarian education from the 1890's to the 1990's

*by John Shotton*

Children experience a series of prejudices from a very early age. Inside and outside of the family they are objects for observaton and adult gratification. Their lives are controlled by their elders, those who have to look after them. While children need some 'looking after' there is a considerable difference between care and complete control. Most young children are rarely encouraged to take decisions for themselves, they are quickly slotted into prescribed gender roles, their sexuality is repressed and they experience no political, social or economic rights.

What the development of a national system of education has done, and continues to do, is to build on this repression and reinforce it. Entry into the so-called educational world is compulsory and regulated. Schools are thus synonymous with education, and for most people are subsequently the only places where any learning occurs.

And yet what is learned in schools is mostly not useful knowledge, but society's required values, attitudes and patterns of behaviour. Attendance and actions are monitored. Autonomy and self determination are usually undermined and a competitive ideology prevails. Two types of child come out of schools, winners and losers, but they are bound by one characteristic, they have been schooled. They are prepared to slot into a society that is similarly schooled. There is a direct relation between the way in which children are perceived, reared and schooled, and the reality of modern industrial economics. Yesterday's children are tomorrow's factory, office, shop and training fodder.

Libertarian education is a theory and practice that recognises these controlling tendencies of national state systems of education. In 1791 William Godwin warned the campaigners for a national system of education in Britain that government would take it over and use it for its own ends. His predictions came true. While we cannot ignore the passion and commitment with which working class people fought for a state system of education that was equal to that of their upper class peers throughout the twentieth century, the fact still remains that it is government who owns the educational system, not the people.

Evidence of this emanates from almost every piece of government educational legislation introduced since 1870. In this context the words of a senior official in the Department of Education and Science speaking after the 1981 inner-city riots are illustrative,

> *"We are in a period of considerable social change. There may be social unrest, but we can cope with the Toxteths. But if we have a highly educated and idle population we may possibly anticipate more serious social conflict. People must be educated once more to know their place." (1)*

This was the backdrop to the Conservative Government's legislation of the late 1980's, the Local Government Act and the Education Reform Act.

There were people who believed that the legislation would give those seeking choice in education far greater opportunities. Some, indeed, anticipated an emergence of more libertarian alternatives. Yet it soon became clear that a concentration of power in the hands of the Department of Education and Science was the primary objective.

Libertarian education has strong roots in basic human rights. It apportions to learners a degree of independence that is grounded in the belief that they can manage their own education. Furthermore it is a set of educational beliefs that seeks to break down the boundaries between teachers and learners, that is grounded in a desire to construct non-coercive and anti-authoritarian pedagogies, and that is not concerned with systems of reward and punishment. It is an all-embracing philosophy of education and learning that is compatible with anarchist views of freedom.

There is a rich tradition of libertarian educational practice in schools in Britain since 1890. This libertarian practice and development has been a product of particular historical circumstances. This is evident in three eras: the period immediately before and after the First World War, a similar period between 1940 and 1950 and the late 1960's and 1970's. All three eras witnessed a considerable debate about the purpose and nature of education, a debate which mirrored a more general and profound questioning of social values.

The first school with a libertarian focus was set up in London in 1891 by Louise Michel. It was called the International School. Following this, Jewish anarchists in the East End of London established a series of alternative schools known as International Modern Schools much influenced by the ideas of the Spanish educationalist, Francisco Ferrer.

The Caldecott Community was also set up in London in 1911, the Little Commonwealth in Dorset in 1913, Sysonby House in Melton Mowbray in 1914 and Prestolee School in Lancashire in 1920. Three very famous and longstanding libertarian schools were set up in the 1920's, Summerhill School in 1924, Beacon Hill in 1927 and Dartington Hall in 1928.

All these schools were born of an idealism that was critical of imperialism, of war, of inequality and that sought a new era. They were also products of communities and individuals who were self-determining, who saw progress lying in their hands, who wanted to put into practice policies and values that society as a whole apparently feared.

Similarly the Hawkspur Camp established at Great Bardfield in 1936, Burgess Hill School in London in the same year, Monkton Wyld School and Kilquhanity House School, in Dorset and Kircudbrightshire respectively, in 1940 and St. Georges in the East School in London in 1945 were conceived in an era that began and ended with fundamental questioning about the horrors and repercussions of fascism. John Aitkenhead, co-founder of Kilquhanity recalls,

*"Similar ideas, similar idealism were motivating soldiers and pacifists alike, only the soldiers had been proved so wrong and so recently. At Kilquhanity we were agin the war but not agin the soldiers, we were agin the government too, and several of us went to jail, for refusing to accept the conditions laid down by tribunals for conscientious objectors. An exciting, stimulating time. Our aim was simple: a school that would be international, co-educational and non-violent."* (2)

Then in the late 1960's and early 1970's, as the young took to the streets in opposition to the Vietnam War and to the constraints of highly prescriptive university courses, there was a similar tide of idealism. This was accompanied by a fundamental examination of the purpose and nature of education. This led to the emergence of libertarian practice in state schools such as Countesthorpe College in Leicester(1970) and the Sutton Centre in Nottingham(1972), and to the creation of a significant number of new, free-standing initiatives, the free schools. There were some twenty of the latter in existence in 1972. As James Jupp wrote at the time,

*"The whole western world is experiencing a phenomenon which*

*had its origins in the United States, the creation of an autonomous youth culture. The basic features of this culture are: that it rejects the adult world, that it is confined effectively to those between puberty and thirty, that it creates its own trends and symbols, that it demands liberation, that it requires less and less adult co-operation for its sub-society to function, that it frightens the adult world to death, and that it is basically harmless despite a dangerous and ever self-destructive aspect." (3)*

"BE REALISTIC, DEMAND THE IMPOSSIBLE", "PUT IMAGINATION IN POWER" - these were the slogans of the Situationists of 1968, they could also have been written over the doors of the libertarian educational projects of the same era.

However, we should not fall into the trap of assuming that all these schools were the same. The libertarian tradition of education and schooling has produced no uniform school, no blue-print. Projects have been the inspiration of individual adventurers and whole communities. They have served different 'categories' of child, different classes, different ages, different cultures. They have, though, been bound by a common approach, a common understanding. At the heart of all the projects mentioned here has been the belief in the capacity of the learner to determine and direct their own learning.

This belief has, in practice, taken many forms. It has dispensed with formal, rigid timetabling. It has been displayed in varying systems of self-government, where the emphasis has been placed on enfranchising learners in decision-making processes. It has rejected common incentives towards, and deterrents against so-called 'good' and 'bad' behaviour, indeed the whole concept of reward and punishment. It has been tied together by a fundamental belief in human virtue.

To attempt a general evaluation of the projects in such a short space is difficult. It is necessary to be aware of the principles they have been based on, to understand the possibilities, to search for and be aware of the problems and to consider their impact.

The principles are clear, they are rooted in libertarian educational theory. A succinct summary of these principles was included in the pages of the early issues of volume two of the magazine Libertarian Education,

*"1. Libertarian Education is against authority.*

*2. Schools and Colleges use their authority to grade and to*

*discipline in order to transform the learners into the sort of products the state demands.*

*3. In contrast libertarian education sees education as liberation. The learner, young or old, is the best judge of what they shall learn next. In our struggle to make sense out of life, the things we most need to learn are the things we most want to learn. The liberated learner controls the process ..., no longer the victim." (4)*

What of the possibilities? Clearly libertarian educational practice has not made inroads into the educational system in Britain, nor into popular educational ideology. Possibilities have emerged, in free-standing initiatives that have been largely self-financing, in independent fee-paying schools, in schools for the unschoolable and in some state schools. Most projects have existed outside of the mainstream, often tolerated rather than accepted.

It is here that the problems of libertarian educational experimentation in Britain lie. While Britain has not had a uniform state educational system, due to the decentralisation of responsibility to local government, it has never afforded much support for alternatives. Consequently funding and support have always been a problem for any projects. This is very different from other European countries, like Denmark and Germany, where state-funded alternatives have been, and are, more common. This has led to other predicaments, namely the exclusive nature of private ventures like Summerhill, or the relatively short lives of the urban free schools.

Many of the projects have dispensed with traditional notions of leadership, and have sought to organise themselves as collectives, without formal hierarchies. This has led to problems of its own; an increased work load for teachers, the accompanying stress and the need to engage in detailed and time consuming processes of induction for new teachers and children.

The pressures on teachers have often led to a failure to address the most basic of questions, particularly pedagogy. As Nigel Wright's book on the early history of White Lion Free School suggests, issues of pedagogy often took a back seat as the day-to-day running of a taxing project took its toll on workers and children alike. (5)

There have been significant issues concerning accountability as well. While virtually all the libertarian educational projects sought to enfranchise all 'participants' in decision-making processes, in the end it was often the teachers who held sway.

Perhaps the greatest problem of the libertarian projects though was their isolation, both from each other and from other potentially supportive agencies. Few of the projects did not face some fundamental crisis in their history. Few of those that did had an extensive network of support. This led to the existence of a tradition of libertarian education and schooling, but never a real movement.

Yet apart from all these problems, what is clear is that the projects have had a considerable impact. In the first instance this has been confined to the participants, particularly to the children. From the International Modern Schools to the free school initiatives of the 1960's and 1970's, child after child has found its experience of libertarian education a liberating one. (6)

However, in exploring the real significance of libertarian educational theory and practice, the most relevant issue is to monitor the emergence of new projects. Recent years have seen the emergence of a new non fee-paying free school in Northampton, a new private adventure, born out of the ashes of Dartington Hall, in Ashburton, Devon, a new, albeit short-lived, libertarian influenced state school in Groby, Leicester and an interesting project for the 'unschoolable' in Leamington Spa. All this reveals evidence of a continuing tradition. Learner-managed learning through libertarian pedagogy lives on.

## References

1. Simon, B (1984) 'Breaking School Rules' *Marxism Today* September p 16
2. Aitkenhead, J (1986) 'That Dreadful School' *Resurgence* Sept-Oct p 8
3. Carr Hill, R (1988) '68-'88 What Went Right?' Lib. Ed Vol 2 no 9 p 6
4. Lib Ed Vol 2 no 1 (1986)
5. Wright, N (1989) *The White Lion Experience* (Leicester, Lib Ed)
6. For details of children's experiences of a libertarian education see Shotton, J (1992) *No Master High or Low* (Leicester, Lib Ed)

John currently works in a small alternative school, part of Bath Place Community Venture, Leamington Spa.

## Learning From Home-Based Education

In the UK and the USA and in various other countries an unusual, quiet revolution has been taking place in the form of educating children at home. At the same time as the fierce debates about mainstream education have been taking place concerning the National Curriculum, Testing, 'Back to the Basics', Opting Out or Opting In, Local Management of Schools, etc, some families have just quietly been getting on with a 'Do It Yourself' approach to education. In the USA over a million families are now 'home-schoolers' as they are know across the Atlantic. In the UK between 5 000 and 10 000 families are estimated to be operating home-based education.

This phenonmenon is more accurately described as *home-based education* because the majority of families use the home as a springboard into a range of community-based activities and investigations rather than try to copy the 'day prison' model operated by the majority of schools. People find this quite hard to grasp and this is shown in the asking of questions about whether such children become socially inept. After a little thought, it is clear that learning activities out and about in the community give children more social contacts and more varied encounters, as well as reducing the peer-dependency feature of adolescent experience than the restricted social life on offer in the majority of schools.

People often try to generate generalisations and stereotypes about families educating the home-based way. The only ones that the evidence supports are:

- that they display considerable diversity in motive, methods and aims
- that they are remarkably successful in achieving their chosen aims

The rich diversity of the home-based education phenomenon is demonstrated by a writing team that includes Julie Webb, Pip Rupik, Bruce Cox, Roger and Tina Rich-Smith, Bernard and Katherine Trafford, Patrick Pringle, Wendy Downing, Roland Meighan, Sue Patullo, Collette Bradley and Dorrie Wheldall.

Schools often take up the posture that if home-based education is to be tolerable, the families should learn how to do it from the 'professionals'. As this collection of writings illustrates, schools may have more to learn from the flexibility of practice of the families, than vice versa.

This book is obtaainable for £5.00 from Education Now, Orders Dept., 109 Arundel Drive, Bramcote, Nottingham, NG9 3FQ

Send for a free leaflet covering many other titles giving a fresh look at education.

## Education Now

**Education Now** is a non-profit making venture, a company limited by guarantee which operates as a publishing co-operative. It currently has five directors who give their services to the company free.

It sets out to report positive initiatives in educations which are occurring in the UK, and overseas, including flexischooling, home-based education, minischooling, small schooling, and democratic schooling. Thus, **Education Now** provides a platform for material and ideas that are fresh and lively. The British educational press often tries to avoid, minimise or suppress such ideas in its apparent anxiety to be seen following the government-led agenda in all its banality. The concern, therefore, is to widen the terms of the debate about education beyond such limitations and short shightedness.

Directors: Ron Biggs, Annabel Toogood, Philip Toogood, Janet Meighan, Roland Meighan.